Psychological
Safety

HBR Emotional Intelligence Series

How to be human at work

The HBR Emotional Intelligence Series features smart, essential reading on the human side of professional life from the pages of *Harvard Business Review*.

Authentic Leadership	*Influence and Persuasion*
Confidence	*Leadership Presence*
Curiosity	*Managing Your Anxiety*
Dealing with Difficult People	*Mindful Listening*
Empathy	*Mindfulness*
Energy and Motivation	*Power and Impact*
Focus	*Psychological Safety*
Good Habits	*Purpose, Meaning, and Passion*
Grit	*Resilience*
Happiness	*Self-Awareness*
Inclusion	*Virtual EI*

Psychological Safety

HBR EMOTIONAL INTELLIGENCE SERIES

Harvard Business Review Press

Boston, Massachusetts

Library of Congress Cataloging-in-Publication Data

Names: Harvard Business Review Press.
Title: Psychological safety.
Description: Boston, Massachusetts : Harvard Business Review Press, [2024] | Series: HBR emotional intelligence series | Includes index.
Identifiers: LCCN 2024010078 (print) | LCCN 2024010079 (ebook) | ISBN 9781647829964 (paperback) | ISBN 9781647829971 (epub)
Subjects: LCSH: Supervision of employees—Psychological aspects. | Personnel management—Psychological aspects. | Corporate culture—Psychological aspects. | Psychology, Industrial. | Teams in the workplace.
Classification: LCC HF5549.12 .P79 2024 (print) | LCC HF5549.12 (ebook) | DDC 658.3/02—dc23/eng/20240506
LC record available at https://lccn.loc.gov/2024010078
LC ebook record available at https://lccn.loc.gov/2024010079

The paper used in this publication meets the requirements of the American National Standard for Permanence of Paper for Publications and Documents in Libraries and Archives Z39.48-1992.

ISBN: 978-1-64782-996-4
eISBN: 978-1-64782-997-1

Contents

Contents

Psychological
Safety

HBR EMOTIONAL INTELLIGENCE SERIES

1

Creating Psychological Safety in the Workplace

An interview with Amy C. Edmondson
by Curt Nickisch

I t was the late 1990s. Medical mistakes at hospitals were a big problem, and researcher Amy Edmondson had a moment of panic.

She had been studying different teams in the same hospital. She wanted to know: Do better teams make fewer mistakes? What she found was the opposite of what she expected.

Turns out, the most effective hospital teams, according to a validated team survey, reported making *more* mistakes, not fewer. She then wondered whether the better teams might not actually be making more mistakes—rather, perhaps they were more able and willing to *talk* about their mistakes.

This study was published in a 1996 paper called "Learning from Mistakes Is Easier Said Than Done," which called attention to how differences in interpersonal climate affected willingness to speak up about mistakes. She argued that organizations could not easily learn from mistakes that remain hidden. To follow up on this incidental finding, Edmondson purposefully set out to study interpersonal climate. This soon led to Edmondson's influential 1999 paper, "Psychological Safety and Learning Behavior in Work Teams." Since then, the research has piled on, showing that psychological safety can make not just teams, but entire organizations, perform better.

Amy Edmondson is a professor at Harvard Business School and author of multiple books, including *Right Kind of Wrong: The Science of Failing Well* and *The Fearless Organization: Creating Psychological Safety in the Workplace for Learning, Innovation, and Growth*. In this interview, she discusses what she has discovered about psychological safety since her original research was published.

Curt Nickisch: *You've learned a lot about psychological safety over the last couple of decades. Now you say it's not the best term. Why not?*

Amy C. Edmondson: The term implies to people a sense of coziness—"Oh, everything's going to be great"—and that we're all going to be nice to each other. That's not what it's really about. It's about candor, about being direct, taking risks, and being willing to say, "I screwed that up." It's being willing to ask for help when you're in over your head.

Why is it that probably more people would say that they don't feel psychologically safe at work than others? It still seems like it's not the norm.

Psychological safety is not the norm at all. In fact, I think it's unusual, which is what potentially makes it a competitive advantage. The reason why psychological safety is rare has to do with aspects of human nature, human instinct. For example, it is an instinct to want to look good in front of others. It's an instinct to divert blame, to agree with the boss. And in hierarchies, these instincts are even more exaggerated.

We want to look good in general, but we especially want to look good in a hierarchy. A spontaneous way to try to achieve that goal is to stay quiet unless you're sure that what you have to say will be well received, especially by the higher-ups.

These are phrases we know, like "better to be safe than sorry," "don't rock the boat . . ."

Right, "don't rock the boat," "no one ever got fired for silence." We tend to play not to lose, right? We stay safe: We want to look good. We want to perform well. Learning is great, but not in front of people. No one likes the part of learning that involves failing along the way.

I want to learn from when that other person does it.

Right, vicarious learning. Do I have to learn firsthand that this doesn't work and have everybody see my failure? I'd rather not.

What's an example of a company that has mastered psychological safety in the workplace and has gained a competitive advantage?

One industry that is very challenging to succeed in—and to do so consistently—is the movie industry. Most companies making movies will have an occasional hit and then a few flops.

Pixar, though, is a company that has had 17 critically acclaimed major box office successes in a row. This is unheard-of success. Ed Catmull, cofounder and longtime leader, worked very deliberately to create and keep creating a psychologically safe environment where candor is expected and possible, especially in the form of providing critical feedback—that is, negative feedback—about a film being made.

They do this in two fundamental ways. One is behavioral, the other structural. For behavioral, Catmull will often say things like "Here's the mistake I made," because leaders have to go first. Leaders must show that they know that they're fallible human beings. Catmull does this when he shows up with humility, curiosity, interest, and acknowledged fallibility.

On the structural side, meetings and sessions are set up so as to design in thoughtful ways to make it easier to give each other candid feedback or to really critique a movie. He'll say things like "Early on, all of our movies are bad. They're terrible." He says that not because that's necessarily good news, but because he wants everyone to know that it's just part of the journey. There is no way to get to magnificent unless they are willing to go through bad and inadequate and sappy and boring along the way. And so they just keep pushing back and making it better.

Let's talk about how to do this. If people want to create a fearless organization, what do they need to do?

There are three temporal steps—three types of activities that you have to do as a leader—but I want to be clear it's not one and done. You have to keep doing them often. The first one is setting the stage, the second is inviting engagement, and the third is responding productively.

Setting the stage means getting people on the same page about the nature of the work we're doing or the nature of the project we're working on. What are the most important variables in the work we're doing? How much uncertainty do we face? How much complexity, how much interdependence? The more the work is uncertain or complex, the more anyone's voice could be essential to our success.

This is where confidence comes into play, right? It's easy to speak up when you know what you say will be well received, especially by the higher-ups. It gets harder if you're not sure and in a complex place— exactly what you're talking about. That just means that confidence levels across the team, across the organization, across the project, whatever it is, are lower, and you have to increase safety so that people still feel that they could speak up when they're not sure.

Right. Each one of us is always setting the threshold for when we will speak up and what we will speak up about. I'm not saying we set this threshold consciously, but rather that we naturally size up the interpersonal context to figure out what seems acceptable. We implicitly calculate the cost-benefit equation to arrive at a place where I might, for example, speak up if I'm 50% confident this is an OK thing to say, in this setting. And maybe for someone else it's 40% or 60%. But we implicitly assess the safety for speaking up about something that is not guaranteed to be a welcome contribution.

"I'll do it once a week."

Yeah. What leaders need to do is just keep trying to push that threshold back down to lower than is natural or instinctive. By reminding us of what's at stake, by reminding us of the uncertainty or complexity, I'm saying, "You know, it really matters. Your voice might make the difference." In doing this, I'm creating the logical case for voice.

What's an example of this?

Julie Morath, chief operating officer at Children's Hospital and Clinics in Minneapolis, Minnesota, emphasized repeatedly that healthcare delivery by its nature is a complex, error-prone system. Why say that? It's obvious, right? Why say it aloud? It's about reminding people of that reality. It's saying, "Things are just as likely to go wrong as to go right. Speaking up saves lives."

Our default mental model is that the work is like work in a factory—the results are all but guaranteed if we follow the right process. With this mindset, people think, "We're supposed to know what to do. We're supposed to execute. We're supposed to hit our targets." And yes, we do want people trying hard to perform well, but when we assume, a priori, that we know what the right metrics are and that everything will go as planned so long as everyone tries hard, we're missing something important. We are missing the actual uncertainty and complexity that lurks around every corner.

Do managers ever run the risk of appearing too soft when they do that?

Many managers worry about that risk. And as a result, they often feel that it's easier to just give the metrics, to appear hard-nosed. But it's also out of touch with reality. The more we're in new, uncertain, or complex territory—and so many organizations are in that kind of territory with at least some part of their activities, especially on the innovation side—the more psychological safety matters. So this is why people, like Ed Catmull, say things like, "We need to hear from you. What ideas do you have? Let's test them quickly."

Or take Astro Teller at Google X: This is a moonshot organization. Most of what they work on probably won't work, but project leaders say things like "We are going to really give it our all. We're going to learn fast in doing so." Leaders who do this well are anything but soft. They're driven, passionate, and compelling, but they're not soft. They do have empathy.

And curiosity—they're trying to understand what's keeping us from getting there.

Yes. They understand human beings. They know what they're asking isn't necessarily going to be easy, so they have empathy for that. But they're not going to give up. There's too much at stake.

What's the next step?

What happens next is realizing that you've got to be proactive as a leader. You've got to invite participation. And what I really mean by that is you have to ask questions.

Ask people directly: What are you seeing out there? I need to hear from you. What ideas do you have? What help can I offer? When I ask a real question, a *genuine* question, and when I listen carefully to the response, I'm creating a moment—and hopefully more—of psychological safety. I'm saying I'm genuinely interested in what you have to say. Maybe what you have to say is a little bit threatening and you're reluctant to say it, but I'm giving you that room to do it.

It is amazing what you can ask somebody if they believe that you care, right? You can ask them anything.

You really can. If they believe you care, they will offer more of themselves, their ideas, their questions, and their concerns, and they will contribute to the situation—and also gain and learn as a result.

Is there ever a danger of too much psychological safety?

I don't think you can have too much psychological safety. You can have people speaking too much, and they need and deserve our feedback. Most people want to be effective. They need feedback about how effective they're being, but it is not a great idea to try to regulate voice through fear.

Does this mean we have to be transparent about everything—like candor?

We have to be transparent about the relevant things. I don't need to tell you about the fight I had with my teenage son last week, but I *do* need to tell you about the new information I just got from the customer. We have to be thoughtful, and get better and better at being thoughtful, in determining what's relevant and what isn't.

What about psychological safety in different cultures? Does this concept still apply in cultures where organizations are more hierarchical?

It's such an important question because it's tempting to say, "Oh, this doesn't apply to places like, say, Japan or countries where power distance really matters, where hierarchy really matters." As tempting as it is, we have to push back and say, "No, it does apply," because the nature of the work is the same. If people in a company are trying to come up with innovative new products, it's just as important to be hearing ideas from people in a high-power-distance culture as in a low one. If a company is trying to do quality improvement on an existing production line, it's just as important that people tell them when things aren't working well. In short, you're not off the hook—even if it's more difficult to create psychological safety in one culture versus another. If it matters for excellence, or for innovation, you've got to figure out a way to create it.

Psychological safety is important for excellence in any organization around the world. It's just harder to get there in some than in others.

What have you learned about psychological safety since you first researched this?

One thing that really surprised me was the Google study—Project Aristotle, which was written up in the *New York Times*. The goal of the study was to find out what distinguishes high-performing teams from low-performing teams. Of course, they included many variables in the research: where you went to school, gender mix—everything you would think of in human capital that might predict team performance.

Nothing worked until they stumbled onto the concept of psychological safety and found that it was a very powerful predictor—in fact, the *most* powerful predictor of team performance at Google.

If you had asked me if psychological safety would be the big predictor of team performance at Google, I would've said, I don't think so. I think all those folks are going to be pretty able to take care of themselves, right? Pretty willing to speak up! They've been told their whole life that they're really smart; they've done well in school. They're going to show up and . . .

They were selected carefully.

Yes. They're going to expect their colleagues to be very interested in what they have to say. So to me, that was quite a powerful and surprising moment. Even at Google, they would have substantial differences in psychological safety across teams, which means that team leadership matters enormously. Team leaders and project leaders can make a team a great energizing experience or a kind of unsafe experience where people are holding back, and that has real consequences for the team.

And that means that if you're at a place where you don't have psychological safety, by trying to be this type of leader or manager, you can make a big difference.

Right, there's such opportunity. There's a lot of latent untapped talent because leaders are not making it psychologically safe enough to get that talent and put it to good work.

AMY C. EDMONDSON is the Novartis Professor of Leadership and Management at Harvard Business School. Her latest book is *Right Kind of Wrong: The Science of Failing Well.* CURT NICKISCH is a senior editor at *Harvard Business Review*, where he makes podcasts and cohosts *HBR IdeaCast.* He earned an MBA from Boston University and previously reported for NPR, *Marketplace,* WBUR, and Fast Company. He speaks *ausgezeichnet* German and binges history podcasts.

Adapted from "Creating Psychological Safety in the Workplace," *HBR IdeaCast* podcast, episode 666, January 22, 2019.

2

Resilient Organizations Prioritize Psychological Safety

By Maren Gube and Debra Sabatini Hennelly

The pandemic, geopolitical instability, and unpredictable markets have made organizational resilience like food in the desert: critical for survival but challenging to grow. By making resilience a strategic priority, leaders ensure that their organizations can stretch and adapt.

Much has been written about psychological safety's role in improving workplace wellness and even in helping stem the tide of exiting employees. But to weather uncertainty, organizations also need to make psychological safety a strategic priority, creating a culture where employees can comfortably raise concerns, contribute ideas, and share unique perspectives.

Three cultural dimensions are critical for resilience:

- *Integrity*: ethical leadership and courageous candor

- *Innovation*: fearless collaborative creativity

- *Inclusion*: authentic respect and belonging

These sustain business continuity, competitiveness, and growth—the intersection of these three dimensions forms the core of a psychologically safe culture. To strengthen resilience, leaders must understand how to connect these three siloed dimensions of culture and develop leadership attributes that encourage candor.

Here, we explain why psychological safety is necessary for the highest expression of integrity, innovation, and inclusion; explore the obstacles to investing in psychological safety; and illustrate how leaders can overcome these obstacles to boost resilience.

Psychological safety as the foundation of resilience

The simple business case for each dimension of resilience is well known. Ethical business behavior (integrity) enhances financial performance; employees who generate and share more ideas improve profitability through innovation; and organizational diversity predicts higher financial returns (inclusion).[1] Both integrity and inclusion are key elements of assessing an organization's environment, sustainability, and governance (ESG) commitments and performance.

Beyond their direct impacts on the bottom line, the three dimensions share an intrinsic connection: Psychological safety is at their core, and any breach erodes their foundation. The fear of retaliation for speaking up compromises integrity, curbing creative ideation leads to stagnation, and disrespectful interactions have a disproportionately toxic impact on engagement and belonging.[2]

Psychological safety does not happen automatically. Because our brains are hardwired to keep us safe, our default mode is to presume some level of threat in most environments.[3] Like animals that sense a predator in the forest, humans tend to stay quiet in a workplace form of "freeze" (from the "fight/flight/freeze" reaction) unless we know we can safely speak up with concerns, fresh ideas, or unique perspectives.

When leaders recognize the connections between psychological safety and resilience, they can model the behaviors that welcome candor—and set expectations throughout the organization to enhance integrity, innovation, and inclusion.

Dimension 1: Integrity

Organizations with a culture of integrity don't sacrifice doing the right thing for short-term profit.

Leaders trust employees to challenge myopic directives, and they empower team members to own decisions that safeguard long-term resilience. Candor is expected, as well as protected, to prevent (or detect and address) legal or ethical issues that could derail or shut down the business.

Two key reasons employees refrain from speaking up are fear of retaliation and a perception that even well-founded concerns will not be addressed. When leaders are committed to encouraging candor, they can be intentional about changing these perceptions.

Early warning signals prevent problems from spiraling out of control. According to research, from 2020 to 2022, 55% of all tips about workplace fraud came from employees.[4] The sooner tips are investigated, the sooner an organization can mitigate related losses. When employees at all levels feel safe to raise concerns, problem behaviors like bullying and harassment can also be confronted in a timely manner.

Retaliation for speaking up about wrongdoing is at an all-time high.[5] The contradiction is not lost on employees, whose companies' codes of conduct oblige them to speak up. Yet, these "upstanders" often face overt or subtle retribution if they do.

Employees who don't have safe internal channels for reporting issues sometimes choose to blow the whistle with the government or the media. Despite the risk of stigma, some find that they have no other alternative.[6] However, external reporting threatens the resilience of organizations in multiple ways. Perhaps the greatest risk comes from the missed opportunity to address the problem in house, early, before the damage escalates.

Dimension 2: Innovation

In a rapidly changing world, continual product and process innovation are necessary elements of sustainable organizational performance. However, the stress of uncertainty reduces individual creativity and diminishes the drive to explore and challenge existing paradigms.[7]

Innovation tends to decline when external risk increases.[8] Focusing on psychological safety internally helps counter that tendency. Embracing "what if . . ." questions fosters a culture of curiosity for generating possible solutions.

The innovation imperative sometimes gets misconstrued as a drive to innovate at any cost. Dissenters can be marginalized and overruled in a new product push, to the detriment of the organization.[9] Putting the brakes on a train that is just about to leave the station requires psychological safety—and is unlikely to happen unless leaders are on board with encouraging passionate dialogue.

Dimension 3: Inclusion

Engagement and belonging are grounded in inclusion. They are foundational to the resilience of not only the organization but also individual employees. In 2021, two-thirds of people who left their jobs said they did so because they did not feel included, valued, respected, trusted, or cared for.[10] Research published in 2022 indicated that almost half of U.S. employees were looking for other opportunities, and the number of women intending to leave was even more startling.[11] Underrepresented (and sought-after) groups were particularly likely to be on the move.[12]

Diversity among employees helps companies anticipate, cope with, and adapt to risk and turbulent conditions.[13] For example, the International Monetary Fund has cited "a high degree of groupthink" (i.e., a lack of diverse viewpoints) as a contributing factor for failing to sound alarms about the impending financial crisis in 2007.[14]

Diverse teams have a broader knowledge base, which allows for better environmental scanning and risk analysis, especially in complex environments. Experiential diversity among team members increases the range of potential coping strategies and leads to better decision-making under threat.[15] The question "What am I not seeing?" is more likely to surface rich perspectives, latent concerns, and novel suggestions when the team is diverse—and when all voices are heard, thanks to psychological safety.

Obstacles to psychological safety

Given the multidimensional benefits of psychological safety, why is it so challenging to make it a strategic priority? Be aware of these two primary obstacles.

Obstacle 1: Blind spots

Senior leaders may not be connecting the dots between different parts of the organization, overlooking the opportunities to work together. For example, functional professionals (legal, risk management, research and development, human resources) tend to focus their requests for limited internal resources vertically in the hierarchy. By competing for support for one-off initiatives—rather than collaborating—they miss the opportunity to help senior leaders realize the cross-functional alchemy of investing in psychological safety.

The onus is on senior leaders to see beyond functions as individual cost centers. By identifying opportunities to champion psychological safety across previously disparate initiatives, they optimize resources for a multidimensional return on investment that enables all voices to be heard.

Obstacle 2: Vulnerability

Psychological safety demands modes of decision-making that are different from what many leaders are used to. It requires leadership attributes like accessibility, humility, and empathy.

One of the most valuable actions leaders in resilient organizations take is to set their personal agendas aside. Many leaders are fearful of feedback that may leave them vulnerable to criticism, but transparent decision-making gets beyond seeing only what we want to see. Input that contradicts our subjective perceptions can be hard to hear but often provides valuable signals for course correcting.

Gustavo Razzetti, culture designer and author of *Remote, Not Distant*, points out that, all too often, leaders claim to have an open agenda and welcome dissent—and yet out-of-the-box ideas and candid feedback are quickly shut down when leaders become defensive. "Even brilliant leaders can have a hard time accepting change, like Steve Jobs when the idea of the iPhone was first floated," Razzetti says. "[W]e need to stop thinking of them as superheroes with all the answers."

Taking the lead on psychological safety

Like trust, psychological safety takes a long time to build—and even longer to rebuild once breached.

Here are five focus areas for leaders who want to make psychological safety a strategic priority in the service of organizational resilience.

Ask questions about the culture

Periodically conduct assessments of engagement, integrity, and other aspects of culture. Pay attention to the results and how they change over time. Take the time to map out existing and desired cultures and design a road map for necessary transformations.

Be clear about your expectations for ethical decision-making and integrity

Silence and ambiguity have consequences. Be intentional about seeking out early warning signals—and clear about responding. Prohibit retaliation against "upstanders"; ensure that employees always have a safe channel for raising concerns and that they know how to access it.

Build trust by extending trust. Align your actions with your words, and show your own vulnerabilities first.

Encourage outside-the-box thinking

Perceived leader support influences creative performance and innovation.[16] Reframe and celebrate mistakes as organizational learning opportunities. Encourage employees to generate and share ideas, which need not always be polished. Welcome dissent without judgment. Assign and rotate the role of "challenger" at meetings.

Invest in and personally support your diversity, equity, and inclusion initiatives

Having even one ally in the workplace fosters a sense of belonging and can encourage people to speak up. Be that ally. Use your relative privilege to share, rather than hoard, power. Foster diversity and inclusion as explicit business strategies, include them in your ESG-related commitments, and tie them to executive compensation. Know how to avoid the pitfalls of disrespectful, noninclusive cultures that make for toxic workplaces with high turnover. Prioritize clear communications, assign projects and roles based on strengths, foster relationships, and invite people to be part of the decision-making process.

Build accountability for psychological safety into performance metrics

Set relevant objectives and provide the necessary training for your managers so that psychological safety rises to the level of a strategic objective rather than a "nice-to-have." Emphasize leadership skills around emotional and social intelligence in career development and promotions. Take the metrics seriously, and hold people accountable.

Also, hold yourself accountable by asking yourself: How am I modeling these behaviors? How can I set up my direct reports to be successful?

Learning to be nimble and resilient in the "new normal" requires an uncommon level of human connection. Understanding how integrity, innovation, and inclusion are connected—and sparking that alchemy—helps organizational leaders *own* psychological safety as a strategic imperative. These three cultural dimensions can map the route to resilience and sustain an abundant harvest, no matter how unpredictable the terrain ahead.

MAREN GUBE is an international speaker whose scientific research on creativity and adaptive expertise has been extensively cited. She is the coauthor of the *Harvard Business Review* article "4 Ways to Spark Creativity When You're Feeling Stressed." Her award-winning insights into why women leave STEM fields drive her advocacy of emotionally healthy, productive workplace cultures. As executive director of Resiliti, her practice is rooted in evidence-based strategies. Connect with her on LinkedIn and learn more at marengube.com. **DEBRA SABATINI HENNELLY** is founder and president of Resiliti, as well as an adjunct professor, keynote speaker, author, and coach. She helps leaders and teams increase trust, collaboration, well-being, and productivity. Her innovative approaches to fostering ethical leadership and cultures of candor—from boardrooms to breakrooms—are grounded in her engineering and legal background and decades of corporate leadership. She is the coauthor of the *Harvard Business Review* article "Bridging Generational Divides in Your Workplace," which is included in *Multigenerational Workplace: The Insights You Need from Harvard Business Review* (Harvard Business Review Press, 2023). Connect with her on LinkedIn and learn more at resiliti.com.

Notes

1. David J. Ferran and Katy Sperry, "Do Company Ethics and Stakeholder Focus Equal Greater Long-Run Shareholder Profits?" Torrey Project, October 25, 2019, https://www.torreyproject.org/post/ethics-stakeholder-focus-greater-long-run-shareholder-profits; Dylan Minor, Paul Brook, and Josh Bernoff, "Are Innovative Companies More Profitable?" *MIT Sloan Management Review*, December 28, 2017, https://sloanreview.mit.edu/article/are-innovative-companies-more-profitable/;

David Rock and Heidi Grant, "Why Diverse Teams Are Smarter," hbr.org, November 4, 2016, https://hbr.org/2016/11/why-diverse-teams-are-smarter.

2. Christine Porath, "The Hidden Toll of Workplace Incivility," *McKinsey Quarterly*, December 14, 2016, https://www.mckinsey.com/capabilities/people-and-organizational-performance/our-insights/the-hidden-toll-of-workplace-incivility.

3. David Eilam, Rony Izhar, and Joel Mort, "Threat Detection: Behavioral Practices in Animals and Humans," *Neuroscience & Biobehavioral Review* 35, no. 4 (March 2011): 999–1006.

4. Association of Certified Fraud Examiners, "Occupational Fraud 2022: A Report to the Nations," https://acfepublic.s3.us-west-2.amazonaws.com/2022+Report+to+the+Nations.pdf.

5. Ethics and Compliance Initiative, "2021 Global Business Ethics Survey Report: The State of Ethics & Compliance in the Workplace," March 2021, https://www.ethics.org/wp-content/uploads/2021-ECI-GBES-State-Ethics-Compliance-in-Workplace.pdf.

6. Meghan Van Portfliet, "Resistance Will Be Futile? The Stigmatization (or Not) of Whistleblowers," *Journal of Business Ethics* 175 (January 2022): 451–464.

7. Susan Peppercorn and Maren Gube, "4 Ways to Spark Creativity When You're Feeling Stressed," hbr.org, October 1, 2021, https://hbr.org/2021/10/4-ways-to-spark-creativity-when-youre-feeling-stressed; Brandon R. Reynolds, "There's A Lot of Uncertainty Right

Now—This Is What Science Says That Does to Our Minds, Bodies," University of California San Francisco Research, November 1, 2020, https://www.ucsf.edu/news/2020/11/418951/theres-lot-uncertainty-right-now-what-science-says-does-our-minds-bodies.

8. Vivek Astvansh, Wesley Deng, and Adnan Habib, "Research: When Geopolitical Risk Rises, Innovation Stalls," hbr.org, March 3, 2022, https://hbr.org/2022/03/research-when-geopolitical-risk-rises-innovation-stalls.

9. Ana M. Fernandes and Caroline Paunov, "The Risks of Innovation: Are Innovating Firms Less Likely to Die?" Policy Research Working Paper 6103, The World Bank Development Research Group Trade and Integration Team, June 2012, https://openknowledge.worldbank.org/server/api/core/bitstreams/32765f05-7a4c-524f-b533-0354984bdb02/content.

10. Mark C. Crowley, "It's Not Just Money. This Is What's Still Driving the Great Resignation," *Fast Company*, March 5, 2022, https://www.fastcompany.com/90727646/its-not-just-money-this-is-whats-still-driving-the-great-resignation.

11. Ryan Pendell, "7 Gallup Workplace Insights: What We Learned in 2021," Gallup Workplace, January 1, 2022, https://www.gallup.com/workplace/358346/gallup-workplace-insights-learned-2021.aspx; "New Deloitte Global Report: Working Women Face Alarmingly High Levels of Burnout Despite Shifting Work Arrangements,

Rise in Hybrid Working," Deloitte.com, April 26, 2022, https://www2.deloitte.com/in/en/pages/about-deloitte/articles/women-at-work-press-release.html.

12. David Rice, "Stemming the Tide: How to Retain Diverse Employees in the Great Resignation," Fair360.com, October 13, 2021, https://www.diversityincbestpractices .com/stemming-the-tide-how-to-retain-diverse -employees-in-the-great-resignation/.

13. Stephanie Duchek, Sebastian Raetze, and Ianina Scheuch, "The Role of Diversity in Organizational Resilience: A Theoretical Framework," *Journal of Business Research* 13 (2020): 387–423.

14. International Monetary Fund Independent Evaluation Office, "Why Did the IMF Fail to Give Clear Warning?" in *IMF Performance in the Run-Up to the Financial and Economic Crisis* (Washington, DC: International Monetary Fund, 2011), https://www.elibrary.imf.org/display/ book/9781616350789/ch04.xml?rskey=anOJuy &result=1.

15. Theresa S. Cho, "The Effects of Executive Turnover on Top Management Team's Environmental Scanning Behavior after an Environmental Change," *Journal of Business Research* 59, nos. 10–11 (2006): 1142–1150. José Orlando Gomes, "Analysis of the Resilience of Team Performance During a Nuclear Emergency Response Exercise," *Applied Ergonomics* 45, no. 3 (2014): 780–788.

16. Teresa M. Amabile et al., "Leader Behaviors and the Work Environment for Creativity: Perceived Leader Support," *The Leadership Quarterly* 15, no. 1 (2004): 5–32.

Adapted from "Resilient Organizations Make Psychological Safety a Strategic Priority," on hbr.org, August 25, 2022 (product #H0771Y).

3

High-Performing Teams Need Psychological Safety

By Laura Delizonna

T here's no team without trust," says Paul Santagata, head of industry at Google. He knows the results of the tech giant's massive two-year study on team performance, which revealed that the highest-performing teams have one thing in common: psychological safety.[1] Studies show that psychological safety allows for taking moderate risks, speaking your mind, being creative, and sticking your neck out without fear of having it cut off—just the types of behavior that lead to market breakthroughs.

Ancient evolutionary adaptations explain why psychological safety is both fragile and vital to success in uncertain, interdependent environments.[2] The brain processes a provocation by a boss, competitive co-worker, or dismissive subordinate as a life-or-death threat. The amygdala, the alarm bell in the brain, ignites the fight-or-flight response, hijacking higher brain centers. This "act first, think later" brain structure shuts down perspective and analytical reasoning. Quite literally, just when we need it most, we lose our minds. While that fight-or-flight reaction may save us in life-or-death situations, it restricts the strategic thinking needed in today's workplace.

Twenty-first-century success depends on another system—the broaden-and-build mode of positive emotion, which allows us to solve complex problems and foster cooperative relationships.[3] Barbara Fredrickson at the University of North Carolina has found that positive emotions like trust, curiosity, confidence, and inspiration broaden the mind and help us build psychological, social, and physical resources. We become more open-minded, resilient, motivated, and persistent when we feel safe. Humor increases, as does solution finding and divergent thinking—the cognitive process underlying creativity.

When the workplace feels challenging but not threatening, teams can sustain the broaden-and-build mode. Oxytocin levels in our brains rise, eliciting trust and trust-making behavior. This is a huge factor in team success, as Santagata attests: "In Google's fast-paced, highly demanding environment, our success hinges on the ability to take risks and be vulnerable in front of peers."

So how can you increase psychological safety on your own team? Try replicating the steps that Santagata took with his.

Approach conflict as a collaborator, not an adversary

We humans hate losing even more than we love winning.[4] A perceived loss triggers attempts to reestablish fairness through competition, criticism, or disengagement, which is a form of workplace-learned helplessness. Santagata knows that true success is a win-win outcome, so when conflicts come up, he avoids triggering a fight-or-flight reaction by asking, "How could we achieve a mutually desirable outcome?"

Speak human to human

Underlying every team's who-did-what confrontation are universal needs such as respect, competence, social status, and autonomy. Recognizing these deeper needs naturally elicits trust and promotes positive language and behaviors. Santagata reminded his team that even in the most contentious negotiations, the other party is just like them and aims to walk away happy. He led them through a reflection called "Just Like Me," which asks you to consider:

- This person has beliefs, perspectives, and opinions, just like me.

- This person has hopes, anxieties, and vulnerabilities, just like me.

- This person has friends, family, and perhaps children who love them, just like me.

- This person wants to feel respected, appreciated, and competent, just like me.

- This person wishes for peace, joy, and happiness, just like me.

Anticipate reactions and plan countermoves

"Thinking through in advance how your audience will react to your messaging helps ensure your content will be heard, versus your audience hearing an attack on their identity or ego," explains Santagata.

Skillfully confront difficult conversations head-on by preparing for likely reactions. For example, you may need to gather concrete evidence to counter defensiveness when discussing hot-button issues. Santagata asks himself, "If I position my point in this manner, what are the possible objections, and how would I respond to those counterarguments?" He says, "Looking at the discussion from this third-party perspective exposes weaknesses in my positions and encourages me to rethink my argument."

Specifically, he asks:

- What are my main points?

- What are three ways my listeners are most likely to respond?

- How will I respond to each of those scenarios?

Replace blame with curiosity

If team members sense that you're trying to blame them for something, you become their saber-toothed tiger. John Gottman's research at the University of Washington shows that blame and criticism reliably escalate conflict, leading to defensiveness and—eventually—to disengagement.[5] The alternative to blame is curiosity. If you believe you already know what the other person is thinking, then you're not ready to have a conversation. Instead, adopt a learning mindset, knowing you don't have all the facts. Here's how:

- *State the problematic behavior or outcome as an observation.* Use factual, neutral language. For example, "In the past two months there's been a noticeable drop in your participation during meetings and progress appears to be slowing on your project."

- *Engage them in an exploration.* For instance, "I imagine there are multiple factors at play. Perhaps we could uncover what they are together?"

- *Ask for solutions.* The people who are responsible for creating a problem often hold the keys to solving it. That's why a positive outcome typically depends on their input and buy-in. Ask directly, "What do you think needs to happen here?" Or "What would be your ideal scenario?" Another question leading to solutions is "How could I support you?"

Ask for feedback on delivery

Asking for feedback on how you delivered your message disarms your opponent, illuminates flaws in communication skills, and models fallibility, which increases trust in leaders.[6] Santagata closes difficult conversations with these questions:

- What worked and what didn't work in my delivery?

- How did it feel to hear this message?

- How could I have presented it more effectively?

For example, Santagata asked about his delivery after giving his senior manager tough feedback. His manager replied, "This could have felt like a punch in the stomach, but you presented reasonable evidence and that made me want to hear more. You were also eager to discuss the challenges I had, which led to solutions."

Measure psychological safety

Santagata periodically asks his team how safe they feel and what would enhance their feeling of safety. In addition, his team routinely takes surveys on psychological safety and other team dynamics. Some teams at Google include questions such as "How confident are you that you won't receive retaliation or criticism if you admit an error or make a mistake?"

If you create this sense of psychological safety on your own team starting now, you can expect to see higher levels of engagement, increased motivation to tackle difficult problems, more learning and development opportunities, and better performance.

LAURA DELIZONNA is an executive coach, instructor at Stanford University, keynote speaker, and culture consultant at Delizonna.com. She specializes in equipping leaders of top companies with the frameworks and tools to build high-performance cultures.

Notes

1. Julia Rozovsky, "The Five Keys to a Successful Google Team," Google People Operations, November 17, 2015, https://www.michigan.gov/-/media/Project/Websites/mdhhs/Folder4/Folder10/Folder3/Folder110/Folder2/Folder210/Folder1/Folder310/Google-and-Psychological-Safety.pdf?rev=7786b2b9ade041e78828f839eccc8b75.

2. Amy Edmondson, "Psychological Safety and Learning Behavior in Work Teams," *Administrative Science Quarterly* 44, no. 2 (1999): 350–383.

3. Tony Schwartz, "Fueling Positive Emotions in a World Gone Mad," hbr.org, November 2, 2010, https://hbr.org/2010/11/three-ways-to-feel-better-abou.html.

4. Daniel Kahneman and Amos Tversky, "Prospect Theory: An Analysis of Decision Under Risk," *Econometrica* 47, no. 2 (March 1979), 263–291, https://kahneman.scholar.princeton.edu/sites/g/files/toruqf3831/files/kahneman/files/prospect_theory.pdf.

5. Kyle Benson, "Transforming Criticism into Wishes: A Recipe for Successful Conflict," The Gottman Institute, https://www.gottman.com/blog/transforming-criticism-into-wishes-a-recipe-for-successful-conflict/.

6. Bradley P. Owens, Wade C. Rowatt, and Alan L. Wilkins, "Exploring the Relevance and Implications of Humility in Organizations," in Kim S. Cameron and Gretchen M. Spreitzer, eds., *The Oxford Handbook of Positive Organizational Scholarship* (Oxford Library of Psychology) (Oxford, UK: Oxford University Press, 2012).

Adapted from "High-Performing Teams Need Psychological Safety: Here's How to Create It," on hbr.org, August 24, 2017 (product #H03TK7).

4

The Two Traits of the Best Problem-Solving Teams

By Alison Reynolds and David Lewis

I magine you are a fly on the wall in a corporate training center where a management team of 12 is participating in a session on executing strategy. The team is midway through attempting to solve a new, uncertain, and complex problem. The facilitators look on as at first the exercise follows its usual path. But then activity grinds to a halt—people have no idea what to do. Suddenly, a more junior member of the team raises her hand and exclaims, "I think I know what we should do!" Relieved, the team follows her instructions enthusiastically. There is no doubt she has the answer—but as she directs her colleagues, she makes one mistake, and the activity breaks down.

Not a word is spoken but the entire group exudes disappointment. Her confidence evaporates. Even though she has clearly learned something important, she does not contribute again. The group gives up.

What happened?

In our previous research, we discovered that teams with high levels of cognitive diversity performed better than those with low levels on these kinds of challenges.[1] In these groups, we observed a blend of different problem-solving behaviors, like collaboration, identifying problems, applying information, maintaining discipline, breaking rules, and inventing new approaches. These techniques made these groups more effective than groups where there were too many rule-breakers or too many discipline-maintainers, for example.

But in the case of the 12 managers in the example we described, they *did* show a cognitively diverse approach. So what happened? We returned to our data to find out. In this team, as well as other underperforming teams, we observed a smaller percentage of the group contributing, longer intervals between testing ideas, and greater repetition of the same mistakes.

The groups that performed well treated mistakes with curiosity and shared responsibility for the outcomes. As a result, people could express themselves, their thoughts, and ideas without fear of social retribution. The environment they created through their interaction was one of psychological safety.

Psychological safety is the belief that one will not be punished or humiliated for speaking up with ideas, questions, concerns, or mistakes. It is a dynamic, emergent property of interaction and can be destroyed in an instant with an ill-timed sigh. Without behaviors that create and maintain a level of psychological safety in a group, people do not fully contribute—and when they don't, the power of cognitive diversity is left unrealized. Furthermore, anxiety rises and defensive behavior prevails.

So the question is, how do you establish and maintain psychological safety with a cognitively diverse group?

The generative organization

Over the last 12 months we asked 150 senior executives from different organizations across the world to rate their organizations in terms of cognitive diversity, psychological safety, and the extent to which they consider their organization able to anticipate and respond to challenges and opportunities, that is, their adaptability. Not surprisingly, adaptability correlated very highly with high levels of both cognitive diversity and psychological safety. We called these organizations "generative," and labeled the worst-performing organizations oppositional (high diversity, low safety), uniform (low diversity, high safety), and defensive (low in both).

We also asked the same 150 executives to choose five words (from a list of more than 60) that best described the dominant behaviors and emotions in their organization. To identify which behaviors correlated with the best- and worst-performing groups, we matched the chosen words with the levels of reported psychological safety and cognitive diversity. Figure 1 shows the most common behaviors selected by each group.

In the Generative quadrant, we find behaviors associated with learning, experimenting, and confidence. Together they facilitate high-quality interaction. Interestingly, "forceful" appears here, too, which at a first glance might seem surprising. Exploring this further, participants were identifying the assertive expression and vigorous analysis of ideas. "Forceful" therefore relates to having the confidence to persist in expressing what you think is important. Psychologically safe environments enable this kind of candor without it being perceived as aggressive.

FIGURE 1

The most successful teams are cognitively diverse and psychologically safe

They also share positive behaviors and emotions.

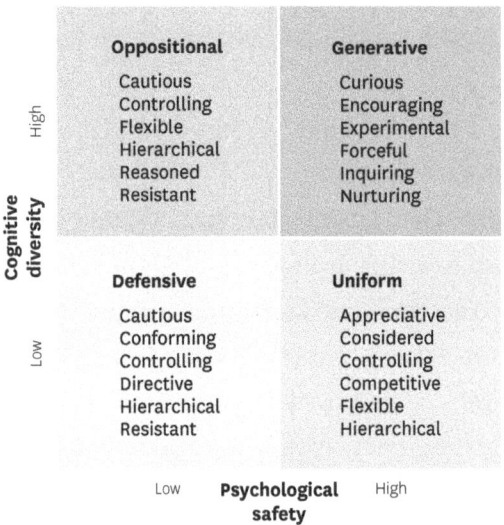

Oppositional

Cautious
Controlling
Flexible
Hierarchical
Reasoned
Resistant

Generative

Curious
Encouraging
Experimental
Forceful
Inquiring
Nurturing

Defensive

Cautious
Conforming
Controlling
Directive
Hierarchical
Resistant

Uniform

Appreciative
Considered
Controlling
Competitive
Flexible
Hierarchical

Cognitive diversity — High / Low

Psychological safety — Low / High

Source: Alison Reynolds and David Lewis, using the Qi Index.

Note that we also see more positive emotions in the generative and uniform quadrants.

By contrast, in the other quadrants, we find words associated with control and constraint. These behaviors are conspicuously absent from the Generative quadrant. We see more negative emotions as well.

The behaviors that count

We choose our behavior. We need to be more curious, inquiring, experimental, and nurturing. We need to stop being hierarchical, directive, controlling, and conforming. It is not just the presence of the positive behaviors in the Generative quadrant that count; it is the corresponding absence of the negative behaviors.

For example, *hierarchical* behavior is cited as one of the top five dominant behaviors 40% of the time in the non-generative quadrants. It is only cited 15% of the time as a top behavior in the Generative quadrant.

This is not because the organizations in the Generative quadrant have a flatter structure—hierarchy is a fact of organizational life—but because hierarchy does not define their interactions. We see *controlling* cited 33% of the time as a top behavior in the non-generative quadrants compared with only 10% in the generative quadrant. We see *directive* cited 24% of the time as top behavior in the non-generative quadrants compared to only 5% in the Generative quadrant.

When we fail to foster a high-quality interaction, we lose out on the benefit of discourse between people who see things differently. The result is a lack of deep understanding, fewer creative options, diminished commitment to act, increased anxiety and resistance, and reduced morale and well-being.

A psychologically safe environment ignites cognitive diversity and puts different minds to work on the bumpy and difficult journey of strategy execution.

How people choose to behave determines the quality of interaction and the emergent culture. Leaders need to consider not only how they will act but, as importantly, how they will *not* act. They need to disturb and disrupt unhelpful patterns of behavior and commit to establishing new routines. To lay the ground for successful execution everyone needs to strengthen and sustain psychological safety through continuous gestures and responses. People cannot express their cognitive difference if it is unsafe to do so. If leaders focus on enhancing the quality of interaction in their teams, business performance and well-being will follow.

ALISON REYNOLDS is a member of faculty at the U.K.'s Ashridge Business School, where she works with executive groups in the field of leadership development, strategy execution, and organization development. She has previously worked in the public sector and management consulting and is an adviser to a number of small businesses and charities. DAVID LEWIS is Director of London Business School's Senior Executive Programme and teaches on strategy execution and leading in uncertainty. He is a consultant and works with global corporations, advising and coaching board teams. He is a cofounder of a research company focusing on developing tools to enhance individual, team, and organizational performance through better interaction.

Note

1. Alison Reynolds and David Lewis, "Teams Solve Problems Faster When They're More Cognitively Diverse," hbr.org, March 30, 2017, https://hbr.org/2017/03/teams-solve-problems-faster-when-theyre-more-cognitively-diverse.

Adapted from content posted on hbr.org, April 2, 2018 (product #H048QY).

5

How Supportive Leaders Approach Emotional Conversations

By Sarah Noll Wilson

The past few years of compounding emotional strain have made it increasingly clear that managers need to shift their focus to meeting and supporting employees' emotional well-being. It's no longer enough to simply provide the operational tools and resources for your team to function—you also need to create psychological safety for them to thrive. That means getting comfortable with having uncomfortable conversations.

It can be hard to know the right thing to say when someone discloses something painful or emotional to you. For example, one of our clients, Evie (names have been changed), an IT manager, suffered through a miscarriage while working from home a few years ago. Her boss, Mike, could tell something was off and called her to check in and see how she was feeling. When he called, she knew she couldn't lie, so she took a deep, courageous breath and shared, "To be completely transparent with you, I want to let you know I am currently experiencing a miscarriage and really struggling with that . . . mentally and physically." Mike was silent for an extended period before finally saying, "Well . . . do what you need to do," and quickly ended the phone call. Mike's reaction has stuck with Evie to this day. In a moment of loss and suffering, she felt entirely unsupported. Was this his intention? No, but it was his impact.

As leaders, it's imperative that we take the time to learn how to show up for our employees, no matter how uncomfortable the situations they face may be for us. For productivity and innovation to thrive, we need to create environments where the team members we serve can thrive. Kelly Greenwood, founder and CEO of Mind Share Partners, and Julia Anas, chief people officer at Qualtrics, surveyed 1,500 U.S. adults in full-time jobs and outlined the benefits of supporting employee mental health in their HBR article "It's a New Era for Mental Health at Work." They write:

Respondents who felt supported by their employer also tended to be less likely to experience mental health symptoms, less likely to underperform and miss work, and more likely to feel comfortable talking about their mental health at work. In addition, they had higher job satisfaction and intentions to stay at their company. Lastly, they had more positive views of their company and its leaders, including trusting their company and being proud to work there.

We heard from a client shortly after the beginning of the pandemic shutdown in 2020 that their leaders were asking them how they were doing more often, but it was clear that they didn't know how to respond to the answers, which varied from "OK" to "Struggling" to "Drowning" and beyond. Checking in is an important first step, but it's how you react to what's shared that creates the ultimate impact. Using emotionally supportive language is an important part of that.

What emotionally dismissive language sounds like

Many leaders aren't aware when they're using emotionally dismissive and potentially harmful language with their employees. What we've seen in the hundreds of leaders we've served is that unintentionally dismissive language often comes from a place of caring. They want to support the person, to help them move through their issue, to minimize their pain.

Sometimes in an attempt to minimize the pain, they minimize the person as well.

On the other hand, some leaders believe that emotions don't belong in the workplace. This lack of empathy can prevent them from understanding who the person is and what they're going through. They ignore the reality that emotions inform decision-making and problem-solving, and they fail to harness the opportunities for growth that emotions can create. Ignoring emotions doesn't make them go away.

Let's look at a few common scenarios that come up when people share mental and emotional struggles:

- *Dismissive phrasing*, such as, "What do you have to be sad about?" or "You shouldn't be sad, you have an excellent job/family/etc."

- *Minimization*, which can be anything from, "Everyone feels like that sometimes" to "There's nothing to worry about."

- *Negation*, which usually sounds like "Hey, it could be worse!" or "That's just a 'first-world problem.'"

- *Prescribing solutions*, like saying, "You shouldn't worry" or "You just need to get more sleep."

- *Toxic positivity*, which may sound like, "Just look at the bright side!" or "Everything happens for a reason!" (A positive perspective can be helpful but can become unproductive when it's the only perspective offered.)

Using dismissive language in these ways can send a message to the recipient that their feelings and struggles aren't real or are unnecessary, and it can even amplify any shame that's already present. If someone is coming to you because they're struggling, the last thing you want is for them to leave feeling unseen, unheard, and unsupported.

What emotionally supportive language sounds like

Becoming a more emotionally supportive leader requires emotional intelligence. Farah Harris, well-being expert and founder of WorkingWell Daily, described emotionally intelligent leaders to me as "comfortable with emotions, whether those that come up within them or come up in others. They create a sense of belonging, because their behaviors allow their team members to be seen and heard."

Emotionally intelligent leaders don't hide behind a shield of detachment when someone presents them with a struggle. They can regulate their own emotions and support others in doing the same.

Here are six ways to be supportive when someone shares an emotional situation or challenge:

Validate their experience

Validation can be as simple as acknowledgment—for example, "I can see why this is exhausting." Especially when experiencing mental health challenges, people can feel alone and even broken. By validating someone's experience, you're not only saying, "I see you," you're also saying, "I believe you," which can bring comfort during a challenging time.

Seek to understand

Give your team member the opportunity to elaborate if they want to. Coming from a place of curiosity can be powerful—for example, "Tell me more about that." When we seek to understand, we're showing the other person that we care about them, want to support them, and want to learn more so we can do more.

Guide emotional and physical support

When someone is struggling, you might ask, "How can I best support you right now?" or "What would be helpful right now?" In a heightened emotional moment, it can be hard for someone to think about or see what may be helpful to them. Asking this question can help them determine and name what they need.

Offer specific support

Sometimes people don't know what they need, may be afraid to ask, or are unsure of what options are available to them. You might ask, "Would X be helpful?" Offering a specific way to support them can make it easier for someone to say yes to accepting help.

Invite perspective instead of prescribing solutions

If you've been through a similar experience as your team member, don't assume you understand

and that what worked for you will work for them. Knowing that someone else has been through a similar experience can be comforting, but everyone is on a different journey. Assuming you know what's best can minimize the other person's needs, centers the conversation on you, and can leave them feeling unsupported. Instead of saying, "I've been there, here's what you should do," try, "Would it be helpful to hear what helped me in a similar situation?"

Acknowledge and appreciate them

Thank your team member for coming to you—for instance: "I can see this has been hard. I am here for you. Thank you for trusting me with this information." This signals to both you and them that conversations like this are important and reinforces a sense of safety for future situations.

Emotional supportiveness in action

As leaders, we often want to help soothe and remove discomfort. If we're honest, there are also times when we want to remove the discomfort not just for our team members, but for ourselves as well. It's not our job to heal, but to make it safe for them to share and to provide whatever support we can. It's OK if you don't know what to say—in fact, simply acknowledging that can be powerful, too.

In 2013, I was diagnosed with panic disorder, which meant I was experiencing repeated episodes of panic attacks. I was new to my company at the time and desperately tried to hide this new challenge and quickly clean up any residual tears before meetings. My company's chief human resources officer pulled me aside and asked me how I was doing. After a pause, she then asked, "How are you *really* doing?"

Standing at the edge of her door so I could escape if I needed, biting my lip and nervous to share, the tears flowed. She listened, validated how scary this must have been for me, and reassured me that the company would support me in whatever way I needed. Finally, she thanked me for sharing. At a time when everything felt heavy, work unexpectedly became a place where things were a little lighter.

As we continue into new chapters of navigating divisiveness, racial injustice, and constant uncertainty, do you want to be the leader who adds to the weight or the one who makes it a little lighter? Learning how to have uncomfortable conversations can help ensure that you're setting up your team members to thrive.

SARAH NOLL WILSON is an executive coach, facilitator, and researcher who is on a mission to make the workplace work better for humans. She is the author of *Don't Feed the Elephants!: Overcoming the Art of Avoidance to Build Powerful Partnerships* and host of the weekly podcast *Conversations on Conversations*.

Adapted from content posted on hbr.org,
March 1, 2022 (product #H06VSM).

6

Five Ways to Reduce the Stigma of Mental Health at Work

By Diana O'Brien and Jen Fisher

Experts tell us that one in four adults will struggle with a mental health issue during their lifetime.[1] At work, those suffering—from clinical conditions or more minor ones—often hide it for fear that they may face discrimination from peers or even bosses. These stigmas can and must be overcome. But it takes more than policies set at the top. It requires empathetic action from managers on the ground.

We count ourselves among those who have wrestled with mental health challenges. Consider this example from our own lives: One morning a few years ago, in the midst of a successful year, Jen couldn't get out of bed. As a driven professional, she had ignored all the warning signs that she was experiencing post-traumatic stress disorder (PTSD). But as her mentor, Diana could see something was wrong. When Jen couldn't come to work, the gravity of the situation became even clearer. In the ensuing weeks, we worked together to ensure Jen got the help she needed.

Diana understood Jen's struggles because she had been there, too—not with PTSD but with anxiety. As the mother of adult triplets with autism and a busy job, she'd often had difficulty managing things in her own life.

Throughout both of our careers, we have moved across the spectrum of mental health from thriving to barely hanging on, and somewhere in between. What we've learned through our own experiences is how much managerial support matters.

When bosses understand mental health issues— and how to respond to them—it can make all the difference for an employee professionally and personally. This involves taking notice, offering a helping hand, and saying, "I'm here; I have your back; you are not alone."

That's exactly what Jen said when a coworker told her that he was grappling with anxiety; it had gotten to the point where it was starting to impact his work and his relationships at home. He came to her because she'd been open about her own struggles. She listened to him, worked to understand what accommodations he needed, and told him about available resources, such as employee assistance programs. Then she continued to check in to see he was getting support he needed and make it clear that she and others were there to help.

How do you learn or teach the people on your team to address colleagues' or direct reports' mental health issues? Here are five ways managers can help drive a more empathetic culture:

Pay attention to language

We all need to be aware of the words we use that can contribute to stigmatizing mental health issues: "Mr. OCD is at it again—organizing everything." "She's totally schizo today!" "He is being so bipolar this week—one minute he's up, the next he's down." We've heard comments like these, maybe even made them ourselves. But through the ears of a colleague who has a mental health challenge, they can sound like indictments. Would you open up about a disorder or tell your team leader you needed time to see a therapist after hearing these words?

Rethink "sick days"

If you have cancer, no one says, "Let's just push through" or "Can you learn to deal with it?" They recognize that it's an illness and you'll need to take time off to treat it. If you have the flu, your manager will tell you to go home and rest. But few people in business would react to emotional outbursts or other signs of stress, anxiety, or manic behavior in the same way. We need to get more comfortable with the idea of suggesting and requesting days to focus on improving mental as well as physical health.

Encourage open and honest conversations

It's important to create safe spaces for people to talk about their own challenges, past and present, without fear of being called "unstable" or passed up for the next big project or promotion. Employees shouldn't fear that they will be judged or excluded if they open up in this way. Leaders can set the tone for this by sharing their own experiences, as we've done, or stories of other people who have struggled with mental health issues, gotten help, and resumed successful careers. They should also explicitly encourage everyone to speak up when feeling overwhelmed or in need.

Be proactive

Not all stress is bad, and people in high-pressure careers often grow accustomed to it or develop coping mechanisms. However, prolonged unmanageable stress can contribute to worsening symptoms of mental illness.[2] How can managers ensure their employees are finding the right balance? By offering access to programs, resources, and education on stress management and resilience-building. In our marketplace survey on employee burnout, nearly 70% of respondents said that their employers were not doing enough to prevent or alleviate burnout.[3] Bosses need to do a better job of helping their employees connect to resources before stress leads to more serious problems.

Train people to notice and respond

Most offices keep a medical kit around in case someone needs a bandage or an aspirin. We've also begun to train our people in Mental Health First Aid, a national program proven to increase people's ability to recognize the signs of someone who may be struggling with a mental health challenge and connect them to support resources. Through role-playing and other activities, it offers guidance in how to listen nonjudgmentally, offer reassurance, and assess the risk of suicide or self-harm when, for example, a colleague is suffering a panic attack or reacting to a traumatic event. These can be difficult, emotionally charged conversations, and they can come at unexpected times, so it's important to be ready for them.

When your people are struggling, you want them to be able to open up and ask for help. These five strategies can help any boss or organization create a culture that ceases to stigmatize mental illness.

DIANA O'BRIEN is an American Marketing Association board member and former chief marketing officer for Deloitte. JEN FISHER is Deloitte's human sustainability leader in the United States. She is also a bestselling author, speaker, and podcast host.

Notes

1. National Alliance on Mental Illness, "Mental Health by the Numbers," https://www.nami.org/mhstats.
2. National Alliance on Mental Illness, "Managing Stress," https://www.nami.org/Your-Journey/Individuals -with-Mental-Illness/Taking-Care-of-Your-Body/ Managing-Stress.
3. "Workplace Burnout Survey: Burnout without Borders," Deloitte.com, 2018, https://www2.deloitte.com/us/en/ pages/about-deloitte/articles/burnout-survey.html.

Adapted from "5 Ways Bosses Can Reduce the Stigma of Mental Health at Work," on hbr.org, February 19, 2019 (product #H04SVU).

7

Getting Over Your Fear of Talking About Diversity

By Daisy Auger-Dominguez

While 27% of chief diversity officers find themselves still having to make the case for diversity, inclusion, and belonging in the workplace, the good news is that the majority of top leaders already understand how critical these efforts are.[1] Indeed, in my work in talent and diversity at Google, Disney, and other large firms, I've found many leaders eager for actionable frameworks and advice to create more inclusive cultures. But again and again I find one thing plaguing their attempts: fear.

These leaders are so terrified about messing up and saying the wrong thing to all their stakeholders—employees, board members, funders, clients, customers—or in the wider world via social media that they're frozen into inaction. Take my experience at Google in the summer of 2015. In the midst of the Black Lives Matter movement, Black employees led walkouts to shine a light on the marginalization and structural inequities they faced in the workplace. Several of my white manager-level colleagues approached me to express their anxiety about how to effectively engage with their employees of color about the protests. Should they say something? Do something? How could they, as white leaders, speak about anything related to the Black experience without offending anyone? Would I look over messages they were drafting for their teams before they sent them? They needed encouragement, permission, and advice before they could do the work of inclusive leadership.

It is critical that leaders not put this work on employees of color but rather visibly do the work themselves. When they don't, they lose their teams' trust and belief in their willingness to lead fairly—and they also set a poor example. I've led inclusion strategy and learning discussions at startups after which founders express dismay that their leadership teams did not participate more actively. If you want your team to stand up for inclusion, *you* need to stand up.

Don't let fear hold you back from this full engagement. Here's what I tell leaders who are afraid of taking a misstep when trying to solve for diversity, equity, and inclusion in their workplaces.

Ask better questions

Genuine inquiry can promote trusting relationships and a safe, respectful, and supportive work environment even in times of complex change. And because you don't have to pretend you're more knowledgeable about these topics than you already are, asking questions can also help you overcome uncomfortable silences and awkward exchanges regarding power and privilege.

This doesn't mean tasking others with achieving your own goals: "How do we move the needle on our diversity and inclusion gaps?" Instead, seek to understand what challenges your employees face every day, especially any practices and behaviors that are causing them pain. Ask questions like:

- What are the biggest barriers to your success, and what role can I play in helping to remove them?

- Do you feel safe enough to take risks at work? To contribute? To belong to the community?

- What percentage of your time is spent on addressing exclusion or microaggressions against you or others?

- Whose voice or what perspective is missing from this conversation?

- How can I help amplify your voice and that of other underrepresented voices?

If you're afraid of making a vocabulary blunder—using the wrong terminology for someone's race, for example, or misgendering people—just ask about their pronouns or what role race plays in how they experience the workplace. Most often you will find that your employees will welcome feeling seen and valued. For those who have been unduly bearing the burden of marginalization and exclusion, though, some questions may trigger deeply held emotions. In those cases, honor whether they want to engage with your questions or not. You can also offer another opportunity to speak if they don't want to do so in the moment.

Show courage not just in what you ask but in how you listen. Suspend your judgment, reduce your instinct to respond reactively, and take time to deeply reflect on what your people are telling you. Demonstrate your interest in the other person's answers, and check to make sure you're understanding them.

As a leader you need to be careful about the words you use, but don't let your fear replace your curiosity.

Read up

There is no playbook for standing face-to-face with inequity, injustice, and oppression while running a business or organization. But there are many resources that can help you better understand the dynamics and the voices at play. Educate yourself on the issues women, people of color, people with disabilities, LGBTQ+, religious minorities, and other marginalized groups face and the compounding effects of intersectional identities.

There are many books on these topics, and the best entry point depends in part on your own experiences.

But a few go a long way. To improve your knowledge and ability to engage in racial dialogue, I suggest Ijeoma Oluo's *So You Want to Talk About Race*. (I focus on race in these recommendations because I find it to be the most challenging topic for leaders to address—and that it's often the root cause of other abuses of power in the workplace.) To better understand the experience of women of color in the workplace in particular, see Minda Harts's *The Memo: What Women of Color Need to Know to Secure a Seat at the Table*. For an exploration of identity, gender, and race, read Jodi Patterson's *The Bold World*. And for a more general look at how to lead in an inclusive way, take up Dolly Chugh's *The Person You Mean to Be: How Good People Fight Bias*.

Lean in to the uncomfortable

As a leader in today's world, you are grappling with complex change on many levels while trying to understand human dynamics that can feel untranslatable, conflicting, and painful. But that's OK.

The only way to address the challenges associated with racism, sexism, and other forms of injustice in the workplace is to be open to experiencing this discomfort in an honest and forthright way. Push yourself to communicate candidly about difficult topics. Accept that you are never going to be perfect. Apologize and admit your mistakes, express gratitude when someone corrects you, listen to those who have been injured or silenced, and commit to doing better. Then pick yourself up, go out there again, and do better.

Your actions as a leader are doubly powerful. In addition to standing up for others yourself, you signal to others that it is safe for them to do so as well.

Just get started

There are no shortcuts or silver bullets for enabling inclusive workplaces. But you need to start somewhere.

Whether it's launching team conversations about white fragility, holding all-hands meetings calling out racially charged incidents when they happen, or introducing yourself with your pronouns, when you take up the work, you can send a powerful message as an ally in a position of power and influence.

DAISY AUGER-DOMINGUEZ is a global leader, speaker, and board adviser, and the author of *Inclusion Revolution: The Essential Guide to Dismantling Racial Inequity in the Workplace*, as well as her upcoming book, *Burned Out to Lit Up: How to Reclaim the Joy of Leading People*. Daisy has led human capital practices and diversity, equity, and inclusion at Moody's Investors Service, the Walt Disney Company, Google, Viacom, and Vice Media Group.

Note

1. "Paving the Way for Diversity & Inclusion Success," Weber Shandwick, September 18, 2019, https://webershandwick .com/news/paving-the-way-for-diversity-inclusion -success.

Adapted from content posted on hbr.org,
November 8, 2019 (product #H05949).

8

The Hidden Power of Workplace Rituals

By Erica Keswin

L eaders are under enormous pressure to address societal issues; maintain an active diversity, equity, and inclusion strategy; and keep employees connected to each other and to the company's mission. And since employees rightly expect to be able to bring their feelings—big and small—to work, supporting employees during cultural trauma and strife is every leader's job. It's not always obvious how to address these issues at work, especially when leaders aren't necessarily trained or experienced in navigating such sensitive, emotional topics. One way to provide the support employees expect is through rituals.

I studied the impact of workplace rituals on individuals, teams, and the bottom line for many years for my book *Rituals Roadmap*. This research has helped me define rituals using two important benchmarks. First, rituals go beyond their practical purpose, moving participants beyond transaction and into meaning. For instance, lighting a candle when the lights go out isn't a ritual, but turning off the lights and lighting a candle at sundown is. Second, rituals are sorely missed when they're taken away.

What follows is one case study from a company that took a risk in real time and created a successful response to a tragedy. Over time, that response became a ritual. Here's how they did it, and how rituals can improve psychological safety, purpose, and ultimately performance.

Time to Connect

In 2022, I met Judith Harrison, executive vice president (EVP) of global diversity, equity, and inclusion at global communications firm Weber Shandwick. After George Floyd's murder, Harrison offered a time for employees to come together to process their grief. Ever since, the company has held the gathering once a month and sometimes more often in response to traumatic events. Harrison calls this simple circle "Time to Connect."

Time to Connect is considered a ritual for two reasons. First, the gatherings aren't directly related to the company's stated mission—their professional communications work. When I asked Harrison what inspired her to bring people together, she told me, "I thought having cadenced opportunities to talk through these events, all of which have mental health impacts on many people, made sense."

Second, as the company's EVP head of brand impact, Lewis Williams, told me, "I'm a fan [of Time to Connect] and I think it can't go away now. . . . Especially with the young employees coming in, it's just a new world when it comes to the employee relationship and what we expect from our employers." In other words, the employees at Weber Shandwick have come to depend on these regular gatherings and would miss them if they stopped.

The Three P's of supportive company rituals

Through my research, I've also discovered why rituals mean so much to us. Time and time again, when it wasn't clear to me why a group or team was so determined to maintain a shared behavior, I discovered that rituals support psychological safety and purpose, which leads to increased performance. I describe this simple formulation as the "Three P's of Rituals."

By applying the Three P's to Time to Connect, leaders can better understand their own rituals—both current ones and those that have yet to be discovered.

Psychological safety

When employees come together for Time to Connect, Harrison begins with some prepared remarks about the world event or topic at hand and then asks the same question each time: "So, how are you doing?"

In order to give employees permission to answer this question honestly, she opens the conversation with her own perspective on the issue. Leading by example provides an opportunity for people to be real themselves. As a result, employees feel safe to respond to the conversations in whatever way works for them—live, in the chat, or via email after the fact.

For instance, after the shooting in Highland Park, Illinois, in 2022, Angela Salerno-Robin, senior vice president of media relations, responded with "I am not OK":

These sessions are a time for us to support one another and talk in a safe space. This time was different. This time, I was the one who personally needed the support. Highland Park is my home. We moved our family here from Chicago to give our children a "safer" place to grow up. It's hard for me to put into words how we are feeling, but I can tell you that as a family, as a community, and as a nation—we are not OK!

It's not uncommon for participants to cry and share out loud or via the chat function. They engage in whatever way is comfortable for them. Not only do they appear to feel psychologically safe enough to do so, but their raw participation creates more safety for others. As chief of staff Jill Tannenbaum put it:

I didn't expect to get emotional on that call, but I was so moved by the humanity and the openness. With a topic that is debated with so much passion and vitriol outside our walls, inside our walls feels safe, enabling a conversation in a way that is immensely supported and always kind.

Ultimately, creating psychological safety starts with leaders' willingness to model it.

Purpose

Helping employees find purpose in an organization is critical to engagement and innovation. One way to do this is to ensure that a company's values are clear, actionable, and widely distributed. Tying those values to key rituals is the perfect way to incorporate purpose into employees' shared experiences.

Weber Shandwick's values of courage, inclusion, curiosity, and impact lend themselves particularly well to making this connection. The ritual of Time to Connect is the ideal way to bring personal and professional purpose together in one very powerful, shared experience based on the company's values. The creation and endurance of this ritual speaks to the courage and curiosity of the employees and company leadership. To be brave enough to take the leap into the unknown and open these challenging conversations is by definition courageous. And to create a forum for people to listen to one another is an expression of curiosity.

Employees have expressed gratitude that Time to Connect creates a safe, inclusive space for *everyone* to share, not only those most obviously affected by the events discussed.

Performance

When I asked Harrison about the business results of Time to Connect, she told me, "Based on people's comments about how much they look forward to the calls and how 'therapeutic' they are, I think the business impact is in engagement, with belonging and trust being subsets of this category." What's more, studies show that community co-creation, a feeling of genuine care, and solidarity have been found to be closely tied to retention.

The numbers speak for themselves. Each month, over 200 people show up—and keep showing up—as themselves, bringing their whole selves to work. Daryl Drabinsky, EVP head of digital health, North America, was so inspired that she initiated "Time to Connect: West" for West Coast employees to connect after *Roe v. Wade* was overturned by the U.S. Supreme Court.

Time to Connect is a powerful example of a simple way leaders can provide the kind of response and support employees are expecting from their companies. Enlisting regular rituals helps leaders offer healing from specific traumas and disturbances while at the same time aligning their workforce with their values and increasing psychological safety and belonging. At a time when the call for authenticity has moved way beyond any brand buzzword, rituals are good for people and for business.

ERICA KESWIN is a bestselling author, internationally sought-after speaker, and workplace strategist. She helps top-of-the-class businesses, organizations, and individuals improve their performance by honoring relationships in every context, always with an eye toward high-tech for human touch. She is the author of the bestselling books *Bring Your Human to Work* and *Rituals Roadmap*. Learn more at ericakeswin.com.

Adapted from content posted on hbr.org,
August 17, 2022 (product #HO76XK).

9

How Leaders Fake Psychological Safety

By Ron Carucci

Hmm, I'm not sure of the best way for us to proceed. What do you all think we should do?"

Josh (names have been changed), the CEO of a global financial services company, said those words to his team during a meeting aimed at solving a thorny problem with a struggling product line. Josh was well-liked and incredibly smart. So smart, in fact, that the team had come to rely heavily on him alone to solve problems. He wanted to change that dynamic so that everyone felt committed to offering their own ideas, challenging his, and sharing in the work of wrestling with difficult issues.

Because of my extensive research on organizational honesty, leaders commonly ask for my help in getting people to be more honest with them. It's a known phenomenon that the higher you climb in organizations, the more sanitized and fawning the information and opinions you receive become.[1] How can you create an environment that welcomes dissenting voices?

Why psychological safety matters . . .

The concept of employee voice—the behavioral science term for the conditions under which people will speak their minds about problems like misconduct or impending setbacks, as well as freely offer ideas and feedback—has been the subject of research for decades.[2] Much of it has focused on dissecting horrific disasters that could have been prevented had someone spoken up (or listened to the person who did speak up). These include catastrophes like the *Challenger*

Space Shuttle in 1986 and the *Columbia* in 2003, which were the result of known issues that had been raised and dismissed within NASA. The groundings of 387 of Boeing's 737 Max airplanes due to mechanical issues beginning in 2019 is another example. Although qualified test pilots and the company's own engineers raised red flags about the new-generation planes, their warnings were ignored by Boeing until two fatal crashes occurred.

In each case, somewhere between the offering and reception of employee voice, things broke down, with tragic consequences.

The critical element that determines if employees will use their voice is the presence of psychological safety. Pioneered and popularized by Harvard Business School professor Amy Edmondson, this is the ability to feel safe acknowledging failure, offering tough feedback, sharing unorthodox ideas, and telling the truth about difficult situations without fear of retaliation. Thanks to her work, psychological safety has mainstreamed into management vernacular. Its importance to high performance is well documented. The consequences of its absence, like the ones cited earlier, are painfully chronicled.

Expectedly, most leaders say they want their people to speak up. And many, like Josh, believe they've made it safe for them to do so, having demonstrated the necessary humility, curiosity, openness, and expressed invitation required to welcome their voices.

But the data suggests we have a long way to go. Research from McKinsey reveals that only 26% of leaders develop the skills needed to create psychological safety for their teams.[3]

. . . and how leaders fake it

One problem, as with any good management concept, is that counterfeit versions of psychological safety inevitably propagate. While most leaders want to encourage people to speak their minds, their underlying (often unconscious) ambivalence about *actually getting the truth* can unwittingly lead them to a performative version of psychological safety.

Here are some well-intentioned but misguided attempts at creating psychological safety I've observed. Each one sent mixed messages that ultimately reduced, not strengthened, psychological safety.

Feigning uncertainty to appear open to others' ideas

One of the best ways to invite others' voices is to acknowledge when you don't know something. This demonstration of humility sends two important signals: first, that it's OK not to know everything, and second, that you need others' help. That's what Josh was attempting to do when he told his team he didn't know the best way forward. The problem was that he was lying, and everyone knew it.

In fact, he knew exactly how to proceed, making his invitation feel manipulative and insincere.

Many smart leaders like Josh struggle with chronic certainty, feeling the need to be the "answer ATM" for all of their team's problems and questions. If that's something you grapple with, acknowledging things you *genuinely* don't know is an important step toward making others feel safe enough to offer their thinking. But for many smart leaders, the fear of receiving lesser-quality ideas than their own makes it tough to ask for them in the first place.

Josh's invitation was met with dead silence. When he and I debriefed afterward, he confessed, "They saw right through me." In the meeting, he sincerely believed he'd done the right thing. His intention wasn't to be deceptive; it was to elicit their ideas. When I asked why he chose that situation—one where he actually knew what to do—to ask for input, he admitted that subconsciously he was hedging his bets. He said, "I guess in hindsight, I wanted an escape hatch if I felt the ideas wouldn't work." Another way of putting that would have been, "If I'd asked for input on something I'm not an expert in, I would have to face the discomfort of considering an untested idea without confidence."

Psychological safety does require some relinquishment of control. You have to jump into the fray of *collective uncertainty*, which initially appears like unformed ideas and inarticulate fragments of genius, with the confidence that great ideas will surface through the *collective intelligence* you harness. Josh thought he was ready for that experience but apparently wasn't. Pretending not to know something to mimic this process is almost worse than pretending to know everything. Both lead to hearing less, not more, of others' voices.

Asking for feedback they don't really want, then not acting on it

Learning to solicit feedback, listen graciously (not necessarily agree), and then act upon it in some way is vital to demonstrating your commitment to psychological safety. If you want those you lead to willingly volunteer their feedback, start by asking for it.

Today, most leaders understand this. Unfortunately, many go about it in ways that ensure they'll never receive it. Here are some real examples of common missteps I've seen recently:

- Waiting until the end of the meeting and then saying, "Anyone have any concerns about this decision? Speak now or forever hold your peace." (The token ask)

- In response to a 360-degree feedback report, saying to someone, "I really want to be a better leader for the team. But this feedback just isn't adding up. Do *you* think I'm this bad?" (Collusion)

- After being told by a direct report that they were too slow making decisions, the leader apologized, then went on for almost 15 minutes describing why they were indecisive, repeating several times how much they appreciated the feedback. (Neurotic deflection)

Most leaders want the benefits of quality feedback; they just don't want the experience of receiving it. Experts agree that one way to get folks to offer feedback is by being the first to acknowledge your shortfalls. Saying something like "I know how driven I can be, and sometimes that can lead me to be insensitive. I'd welcome your help in making sure I'm not pushing too hard" helps people trust that your recognition of the issue means you want to change.

But here, too, I've seen leaders twist this tactic. In one organization, I observed another manager, Phoebe, "admit" her leadership gaps in the form of a tearful, self-deprecating rant about how horrible she was. Not only did she *not* get honest feedback about how she could improve, but the team felt guilted into giving her false reassurance that she was a great leader. This simply reinforced the team's conclusion that Phoebe couldn't take honest feedback.

If you find that you're feedback averse, get to the bottom of why. Ask yourself, "What's my worst nightmare about hearing how my team truly feels about my leadership?" Maybe you aren't as capable in some areas as you thought. Maybe the gap between your intent and your impact is wider than you considered. Maybe they can't stand you. Regardless, isn't it better to know than to perpetuate the illusion that things are better than they are?

When you solicit feedback to appear as though you care, without a commitment to changing, you're fooling only yourself. All you accomplish is convincing people that you're not capable of hearing the truth—about anything. So when your team faces something devastating that they *could* warn you about, the loss of psychological safety your pretend-feedback invitation caused is going to come back to bite you.

Responding to failure
with artificial compassion

Most leaders understand that making it safe to admit errors is vital to great performance, especially in complex work where mistakes can have substantial consequences. So in the face of an admitted mistake, harsh blaming behaviors like screaming, berating, or being excessively punitive will only ensure that future mistakes get swept under the carpet.

But what does responding *effectively* to failure look like? It requires some combination of caring accountability that protects the dignity of people responsible for the mistake, as well as remedying the error when possible, or at least ensuring that learnings are applied to prevent it from happening again.

The confluence of emotions leaders experience upon hearing about unforeseen errors can be hard to completely mask. Reactions like surprise (*How could this have happened?*), panic (*What's the fallout? How will this make me look? Am I complicit?*), disappointment (*I was counting on this project going smoothly*), and even anger (*I warned them this could happen*) can make it awfully hard to center responses like curiosity, compassion, and dignified accountability. And when well-intended leaders try to mask those reactions, it creates a foul mix of awkward behaviors that mistake-makers receive just as harmfully as if the leader had shouted and disgraced them.

One employee told me, "I wish he'd just yelled at me and gotten it over with. It would have felt more honest. I could tell he was trying to look sympathetic by asking questions and appearing supportive. He said the right words. But he was wringing his hands, his face was tight with tension, and his tone felt condescending and cold, like he was reading a script."

Clearly this manager's good intentions backfired. He had caused the very feelings he believed he was preventing. Suppressing our feelings is different than regulating them. Leaders must learn to regulate intensified emotions honestly while still focusing on the person and the failure. While admittedly difficult, it is possible to judiciously express your emotions while caring for an employee who's failed and supporting them through the experience. Trying to disguise strong emotions only discharges them.

———————

When it comes to psychological safety, leaders want the best of all worlds: All voices heard and considered, failure acknowledged and learned from, and feedback offered clearly and received graciously. But they also want harmony, comfort, and a sense of equilibrium. The good news is that you can have both—you just can't have one without the other. The only way to harmony, comfort, and equilibrium is *through* the messiness of disagreement, the emotional discomfort that accompanies hard news, and the disequilibrium that arrives when failure must be courageously and compassionately engaged. Persevering through that journey creates real psychological safety—one management skill for which "fake it till you make it" definitely doesn't work.

RON CARUCCI is a cofounder and managing partner at Navalent, working with CEOs and executives pursuing transformational change. He is the bestselling author of eight books, including *To Be Honest* and *Rising to Power*. Connect with him on LinkedIn @RonCarucci.

Notes

1. Janis Skrastins and Vikrant Vig, "How Organizational Hierarchy Affects Information Production," *Review of Financial Studies* 32, no. 2 (February 2019): 564–604.
2. Elizabeth W. Morrison, "Employee Voice and Silence," *Annual Review of Organizational Psychology and Organizational Behavior* 1, no. 1 (2014): 173–197.
3. "Just 26 Percent of Leaders Create Psychological Safety for Their Teams," McKinsey & Company, February 24,

2021, https://www.mckinsey.com/featured-insights/
sustainable-inclusive-growth/chart-of-the-day/just-26
-percent-of-leaders-create-psychological-safety-for-their
-teams.

Adapted from content posted on hbr.org,
December 5, 2023 (product #H07X93).

10

To Help Your Team Grow, Give Them Space to Struggle

By Kelli Thompson

H ow are you justifying the sales and expenses estimates?" the CEO asked. My face glowed red as I stuttered. My heart rate skyrocketed, and my throat tightened. I looked at my boss, Valerie. She made eye contact, held a soft gaze, and said nothing.

She could have eased some of the heat directed my way by chiming in and saving me, but she didn't. That's because I had asked Valerie for an opportunity to present to our organization's leadership team. Prior to the meeting, she'd informed the head of our banking division and the CEO that I was taking on this stretch assignment and that she would be an observer.

So instead of taking over from me when I was facing tough questions, she let me figure my own way out of the discomfort. I did muddle through it, albeit not as well as I would have liked, but in a way that left me better prepared for my next meeting with him.

I remember Valerie as a good boss because she often gave me developmental opportunities like these. The stakes were usually low like that small, internal meeting, where everyone knew I was still green and would be supportive. Valerie was present but in the background, allowing me to succeed or stumble but learn from the experience either way. Afterward, she never gave me long lists of suggestions on how to improve. Instead, she asked great questions that prompted me to think about what I could have done differently.

In theory, most leaders know how important it is to delegate challenging tasks to employees both to help them grow and to create a collaborative, empowered, productive team. But faced with real workplace demands, it can be tough to put this into practice. Many of my clients say things like "I'm the only one who can do the job" or "If this project doesn't go smoothly, the whole team will suffer."

Empathy can get in the way, too. When you see an employee struggling, it's only natural to want to step in and help. But from the other side, this can feel more like micromanagement than support. And when leaders overfunction by keeping too many tasks, they allow their teams to underfunction.

Here are some strategies you can use to make delegation easier.

Shift from doer to leader mindset

In my corporate job, we promoted the best doers into leaders. This came with an assumption that they would magically shift from being good at and motivated by performance excellence and rewards to excelling at and caring deeply about developing others' potential. The mindset shift may be the hardest part of all. So how can you facilitate this in yourself?

- *Notice your payoff from* doing. The thrill of achievement provides a quick dopamine hit.[1] But that's something you need to resist to get to the greater fulfillment of having helped others improve.

- *Claim your leadership identity by getting clear on values.* Ask yourself: What three words do I want people to use to describe my leadership style? For example: Do I want to lead with control, urgency, and expertise? Or with patience, curiosity, and empowerment?

- *Be intentional about responding, not reacting.* In the moments where you are triggered to step in, ask yourself: Would that be aligned with my values and who I want to become as a leader?

Embrace the discomfort
of the learning process

Many leaders tell me that, after witnessing an employee falter, taking back the work felt like the most supportive thing to do. I've felt this tension too. But Valerie taught me the power of holding space for struggle. Yes, this creates discomfort for both leader and employee because it's a new way of working for everyone. However, as Gallup reminds us, one of the keys to engagement at work is the opportunity for stimulating challenges.[2] And when you push through the struggle, the result is growth for all parties.

How can you embrace, rather than resist, the discomfort of learning?

- *Name your emotions.* According to psychologist Susan David, doing so offers clarity and resilience and can empower you to respond in an intentional way, aligned with your values.[3]

- *Normalize being uncomfortable.* Neuroscientists know that these are the periods in which learning happens and perseverance is developed.[4]

- *Reframe the situation.* One potential reframe is "I was allowed to struggle, and that's where I gained confidence in my skills. So I'm going to give my employee the same gift of time to solve the problem on their own."

Distinguish between high- and low-stakes tasks

Leaders often tell me they remain stuck as doers because employees make too many high-impact mistakes that require intervention. But this usually happens when the bosses themselves hold on to all the work for far too long and are then forced to delegate at the wrong moment. The key is to instead hand off tasks when the stakes are low and missteps tolerated, or even expected.

What makes an environment low-stakes? Failure will support learning more than it would hurt reputation. Mistakes will not impact team or company success. The environment is safe for stops and do-overs. The people involved have support and compassion for less experienced colleagues on learning curves.

To know which tasks are ripe for delegation, consider ones that now feel easy or rote to you but would be good development opportunities for those on your team. Also think about work that drains your energy and doesn't align with your skills, talents, and strengths but might excite and feel like a perfect fit for others.

For example, if your employee's goal is to develop better presentation skills, suggest a low-stakes activity like asking them to lead the next staff meeting before offering them a high-stakes one like conducting a client meeting. Or if they want to get better at influencing others, challenge them to get buy-in from a small team on using a new tool or work process before asking them to persuade your whole division to implement it.

Be curious and facilitative

Early in my corporate career as a trainer, people told me that I was visibly nervous during sessions I was leading. I explained to my boss that I was worried about not having answers to participants' questions. Her response: "What if your role isn't to have all the answers but to facilitate the expertise in the room?" This changed my perspective.

Like trainers, leaders can't be expected to have all the answers. But they do need to have patience and curiosity and ask insightful questions that will facilitate learning. For example: What has your current approach been? Can you apply past experience to this problem? What is this situation teaching you?

Finally, practice compassion and grace. This doesn't mean tolerating poor effort or careless mistakes. Instead, it means offering understanding and accommodation in the face of someone not doing something exactly how you would do it.

Valerie's approach that day with our CEO didn't feel good at the time. But had she intervened, I wouldn't have learned how to respond to unexpected questions or later reflected on how to better prepare for executive presentations. If she'd followed up with advice, I wouldn't have discovered my own authentic ways of improving. To this day, I credit her with helping me to develop the ability to present calmly in high-stakes situations. She's also the reason I have the courage to delegate to colleagues and team members, even if it means watching them struggle. That's the only way that all of us—leaders and employees—grow.

KELLI THOMPSON is a women's leadership coach and speaker. She is the founder of the Clarity and Confidence Women's Leadership Program, and a Stevie Award winner for Women in Business—Coach of the Year. She is the author of *Closing the Confidence Gap: Boost Your Peace, Your Potential, and Your Paycheck.*

Notes

1. "The Neuroscience of Achievement," Noesis, November 19, 2019, https://www.noesislearning.com/2019/11/19/the-neuroscience-of-achievement/.
2. Ben Wigert, "The Top 6 Things Employees Want in Their Next Job," Gallup Workplace, February 21, 2022, https://www.gallup.com/workplace/389807/top-things-employees-next-job.aspx.
3. Susan David, "3 Ways to Better Understand Your Emotions," hbr.org, November 10, 2016, https://hbr.org/2016/11/3-ways-to-better-understand-your-emotions.
4. Rishi Sriram, "The Neuroscience Behind Productive Struggle," Edutopia, April 13, 2020, https://www.edutopia.org/article/neuroscience-behind-productive-struggle/.

Adapted from content posted on hbr.org,
July 6, 2023 (product #H07PLS).

Index